Let's Go! Let's Grow!

WHAT IS HATCHING?

Stephanie Anne Box

Rourke
Educational Media

A Division of
Carson Dellosa Education

T0020117

BEFORE AND DURING READING ACTIVITIES

Before Reading: *Building Background Knowledge and Vocabulary*

Building background knowledge can help children process new information and build upon what they already know. Before reading a book, it is important to tap into what children already know about the topic. This will help them develop their vocabulary and increase their reading comprehension.

Questions and Activities to Build Background Knowledge:

1. Look at the front cover of the book and read the title. What do you think this book will be about?
2. What do you already know about this topic?
3. Take a book walk and skim the pages. Look at the table of contents, photographs, captions, and bold words. Did these text features give you any information or predictions about what you will read in this book?

Vocabulary: *Vocabulary Is Key to Reading Comprehension*

Use the following directions to prompt a conversation about each word.
- Read the vocabulary words.
- What comes to mind when you see each word?
- What do you think each word means?

Vocabulary Words:
- *climates*
- *clutch*
- *cold-blooded*
- *embryo*

During Reading: *Reading for Meaning and Understanding*

To achieve deep comprehension of a book, children are encouraged to use close reading strategies. During reading, it is important to have children stop and make connections. These connections result in deeper analysis and understanding of a book.

Close Reading a Text

During reading, have children stop and talk about the following:
- Any confusing parts
- Any unknown words
- Text to text, text to self, text to world connections
- The main idea in each chapter or heading

Encourage children to use context clues to determine the meaning of any unknown words. These strategies will help children learn to analyze the text more thoroughly as they read.

When you are finished reading this book, turn to the last page for an **After-Reading** activity.

Table of Contents

Who Lays Eggs?

What do you think will hatch from these eggs?

Cold-blooded animals, like reptiles and fish, lay eggs. Birds, who are warm-blooded, also lay eggs. Eggs can be many different sizes and colors. Eggs can be hard, soft, jelly-like, or leathery.

Animals lay eggs in a **clutch**. Clutches can be hundreds of eggs or just a few. Can you identify a clutch in each picture?

It's Time to Lay

Animals lay eggs in many different places. They lay eggs in water, nests, and even underground. Animals lay eggs in warm and cold **climates**.

Where is the coldest place eggs are laid?

Some parents warm the eggs. They stay with the eggs until they hatch.

Other animal parents leave after they lay their eggs.

Did you know that some parents stay with their young after they hatch? Other animals are born knowing what to do. After they hatch, they do not need their parents.

Waiting to Hatch

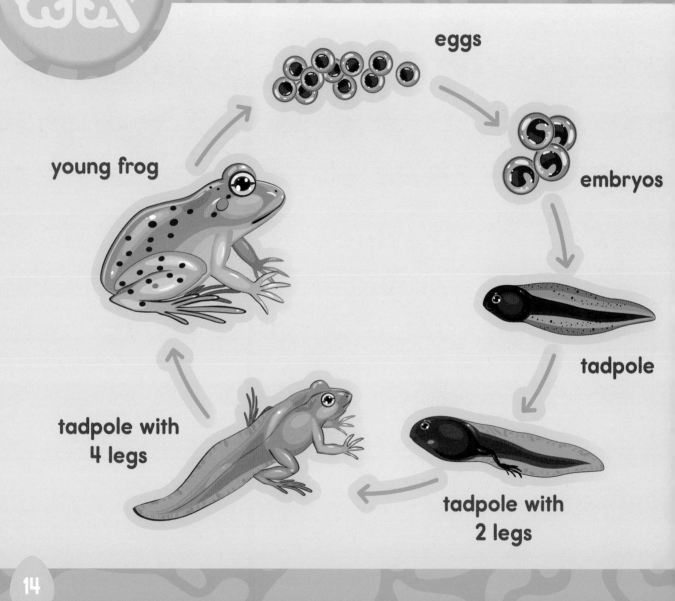

eggs

embryos

tadpole

tadpole with 2 legs

tadpole with 4 legs

young frog

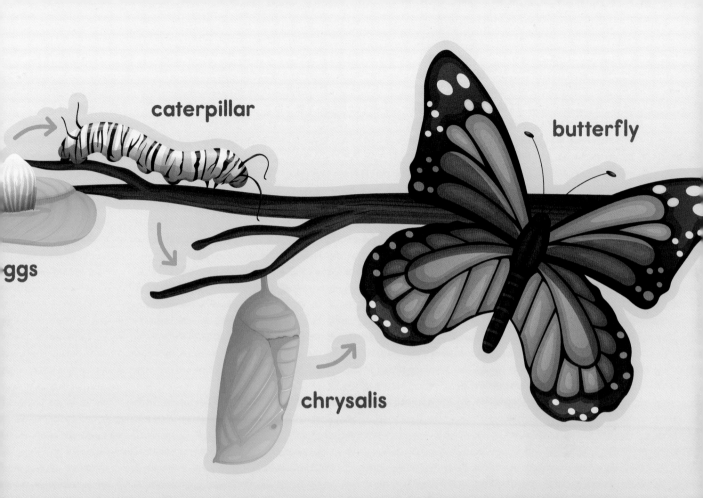

caterpillar

butterfly

ggs

chrysalis

If an egg is fertilized, an **embryo** begins to form. Some animals hatch and then go through stages to become an adult.

Some animals need more time to develop while inside the egg. Some eggs hatch in days, while others take weeks or months.

1 Day 5 Days 15 Days

When the animal is ready to hatch, the young will use its egg tooth to break out of the egg.

Look what hatched! Remember the eggs at the beginning? Did you guess what would hatch?

Photo Glossary

climates (KLYE-mit): The types of weather typical of a place over a long period of time.

clutch (kluhch): A nest of eggs.

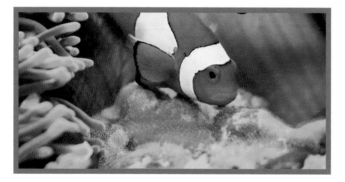

cold-blooded (kohld-BLUHDid): Having a body temperature that changes according to the temperature of the surroundings, like reptiles or fish.

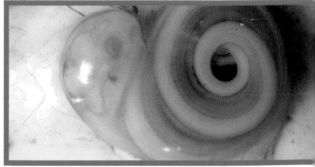

embryo (em-BREE-oh): A human baby, animal, or plant in the very early stages of development before birth.

Activity: Draw a Life Cycle

Imagine you found a mysterious, colorful egg. What kind of animal might hatch from an egg like this? Use what you know about animals that hatch from eggs to design a new, make-believe animal. Draw a picture to show the animal's life cycle and how it grows inside the mysterious egg. Write three characteristics that this new animal shares with animals you learned about in this book.

Items Needed:

paper
pencil
crayons/markers

Index

About the Author

Stephanie Anne Box loves all kinds of baby animals, especially those that hatch from eggs. Stephanie is a kindergarten teacher who lives in Mississippi with her husband Josh, and her dog, Dudley.

After-Reading Activity

Think about your favorite animals. Did they hatch from eggs? If so, find out what kind of eggs they lived in before they hatched. Were they hard and blue? Were they leathery, long, and white?

Library of Congress PCN Data

What Is Hatching? / Stephanie Anne Box
(Let's Go! Let's Grow!)
ISBN 978-1-73165-176-1 (hard cover)(alk. paper)
ISBN 978-1-73165-221-8 (soft cover)
ISBN 978-1-73165-191-4 (e-Book)
Library of Congress Control Number: 2021944776

Rourke Educational Media
Printed in the United States of America
01-3402111937

© 2022 Rourke Educational Media

www.rourkeeducationalmedia.com

Edited by: Laura Malay
Cover design by: Tammy Ortner
Interior design by: Tammy Ortner
Photo Credits: Cover p 1 © MP_P, © AVN Photo Lab, © Ivaylo Ivanov, © Filip Dokladal, © Katharina Scharle, p 4 © NivCube, p 5 © Betsy Cooley / EyeEm, p 6 © beckysphotos, © cckbest, p 7 © 7innaMamap 8 © Martin Smart, p 9 © sujesh, p 10 © Brandon B, p 11 Danita Delimont, © p 12 © Jarib, p 13 © Cora Unk Photo, p 14 © Kazakova Maryia, p 15 © BlueRingMedia, p 16 © sunit paenphat, © COULANGES, p 17 © BlueRingMedia, © Silarock, p 18 © Heiko Kiera, p 19 © Somedaygood, p 20 © Gregory Rees, p 21 © unpetitgraindefolie, p 22 © Martin Smart, © beckysphotos, © sujesh © COULANGES, p 24 © Joan Peno McCool